DAINTREE
CAPE TRIBULATION

PETER LIK

WILDLIFE PHOTOGRAPHY
MICHAEL CERMAK

"My total dedication and obsession
with photography has taken me on
journeys into many remarkable areas
throughout Australia.
I captured much of this collection of
images using a specialist panoramic
camera. Because of the wider field
of view, this format enables me to
portray the true spirit of Australia on
film. Upon viewing these images
I am sure you will share with me the
tranquillity and solitude I experienced
whilst exploring the stunning beauty
of this country."

 PETER LIK PUBLISHING

Telephone: 1300 364 391

CAIRNS
PO Box 2529 Cairns Queensland 4870 Australia
Telephone: (07) 4053 9000   **Fax:** (07) 4032 1277
sales@peterlik.com.au

peterlik.com

© **Peter Lik Publishing** BK14
ISBN 1 876585021

Front cover - Aerial view of Cape Tribulation
Back cover - Ringtail possum
Title Page - Twilight, Thornton's Beach

As you walk through the Daintree Rainforest, it is easy to understand how Christopher Columbus described the first rainforest he encountered as "The Garden of Eden". Protected from the sun by a roof of enormous palms, trees and curling, twisting vines, you cannot help but notice the multitude of sounds, scents, and most of all life. Rainforests have remained basically unchanged for millions of years, yet so little is really known about their inhabitants - from the largest climbing mammal to the tiniest soil-dwelling insect.

Australia's tropical rainforests stretch in a narrow belt along the north-eastern coast between Townsville and Cooktown, yet cover less than 1% of Australia's land area. They are part of what is called the Wet Tropics World Heritage Area of North Queensland, aimed at protecting, conserving, rehabilitating and most of all transmitting this wonderful environment to future generations. They boast some of the most rugged topography, fast flowing rivers, deep gorges and spectacular waterfalls in Australia, as well as a rich diversity of plant and animal life, including 65% of Australia's fern species and 60% of native butterfly species. The association of the fringing coral reefs and rainforested coastline in the Cape Tribulation area is unparalleled anywhere in the world, and a section between Cooktown and Cardwell contains the only recognised Australian Aboriginal rainforest culture.

In 1994, the federal government funded a $23 million Daintree Rescue Programme to help protect the area. The government has since bought back over 1600 hectares of privately owned land

Cape Tribulation surrounded by fringing reefs.

Previous Page: Cape Tribulation beach reflects its beauty over the Coral Sea.

Aerial view of the palm fringed beach of Cape Tribulation.

The unique Daintree River ferry crossing.

Exploring the Daintree and Bloomfield track is a real adventure. The journey starts with the Daintree River Ferry crossing where crocodiles can often be spotted. Continuing north, the crystal clear water of Coopers and Noah Creek are crossed before reaching the famous Cape Tribulation headland.

Exploring the Bloomfield track.

M. Cermak

*S*alt-water crocodiles are found in most creeks, rivers and billabongs throughout the Daintree region. They are by no means restricted to salt water (as their name may suggest) but inhabit salt, brackish and fresh water environments. Though these reptiles are shy and secretive in habit, large individuals may not discriminate between unsuspecting tourist and the next meal.

M. Cermak

Cow Bay.

A tidal pool at Coopers Creek estuary with the cloud shrouded Thorntons Peak in the background.

The sun's first rays illuminate tidal sand patterns at the mouth of Coopers Creek.

A long time-exposure captures the mood at Thorntons Beach.

Looking north along the Bloomfield coastline.

Pandanus fruit.

Pandanus palms frame the Cape Tribulation headland.

𝒰pon crossing the Daintree River, you will experience the magnificent beaches and lush rainforests that people have come from all over the world to admire. This is Australia's largest remaining stand of tropical lowland rainforest - a last refuge for unique plants and animals with a history of over 140 million years.

At the onset of the monsoonal rains the Daintree rainforest echoes with frog choruses like this Dainty Green Tree Frog.

M. Cermak

The Paradise Kingfisher is a regular visitor to the Daintree. These birds arrive from Central New Guinea in November each year to breed.

M. Cermak

To many, Praying Mantids and Stick Insects are confusing because of their similar appearance. While Mantids like this "Hooded Horror Mantid" are ferocious predators, Stick Insects feed on leaves. Most species are generalists in their diet but this Peppermint Stick Insect specializes on Pandanus plants.

M. Cermak

The Daintree rainforests are inhabited by many species of geckos, however, this Giant Gecko is found near the tip of Cape York.

A bird's-eye view of the rainforest canopy.

The Tropic Sunbird

$\mathcal{T}$he most famous of Australia's lowland rainforest lies north of the Daintree River in North Queensland and is protected as a National Park. This steamy landscape usually occurs along the the coast in the wettest places, where rainfall is typically between 1600mm and 5000mm per year. Towering trees with large leafs and broad leafed palms are characteristic of lowland rainforests.

Strangler fig tree, Marrdja boardwalk.

A fig tree stands proudly on the forest floor.

It is like a optical illusion when the sunrays hit the iridescent blue wings of the Ulysses Butterfly while flying fast through the rainforest.

Daintree River mouth captured from the Alexandra Range lookout.

Palm Valley provides a unique umbrella-like canopy of Licuala Palms.

The Brown Antechinus is commonly called the "Marsupial mouse". This cute nocturnal predator is a true marsupial with a pouch.

Reef meets rainforest, Coconut Beach.

Cow Bay.

Early morning skies, Cape Tribulation.

Bloomfield Falls.

On a sunny day the rainforest becomes alive with butterflies. The Macleay's Swallowtail prefers higher altitudes in the tropics and oddly enough, it can be also found in the Australian Alps during the summer months.

M. Cermak

ifferent animals adopted different strategies of avoiding potential predators. Hanging upside down on thin branches gives the Spectacled Flying-Fox some protection against non-climbing predators, while the Harlequin Bug relies on it's bright, defensive colouration. Like all possums, the Common Ringtail is a nocturnal herbivore and it pays to stay alert while foraging amongst the branches.

Enveloped in cloud, highland rainforests are amongst the most ancient on earth.

Sunglow during a late afternoon rainstorm.

Previous Page: Mossman Gorge.

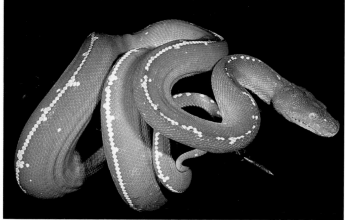

M. Cermak

M. Cermak

$\mathcal{T}$ropical rainforests comprise complexity of colours, textures, shapes and contrasts. Because of this, many animals that inhabit such an environment, are quite inconspicuous and difficult to see, despite of their bright colours. This unusual blue colouration of the Common Green Tree Frog is caused by the lack of yellow pigment in the skin cells and such individuals are extremely rare. The magnificent Green Pythons are only found in the Iron and McIlwraith Ranges on Cape York. The red colour of some rainforest mushrooms signifies one thing - not edible!

The Papuan Frog Mouth Owl feeds mainly on insects.

The Jabiru is Australia's only true stork.

The Cassowary, Australia's largest bird is flightless and feeds on rainforest fruits.

M. Cermak

If anything is to remind us of the Jurassic fauna, then the Boyd's Forest Dragon has to be it.

The Orange-thighed Tree Frogs spend their entire lives up in the tops of rainforest trees where they hide amongst epiphytes.

M. Cermak

Licuala palms fringe Coopers Creek.

Overleaf: The Great Barrier Reef.

Tranquil stream, Daintree Rainforest.

Azure waters of Coconut Beach contrast against a superb backdrop of World Heritage mountains.

East Hope Island, north east of Cape Tribulation is an idyllic coral atoll.

"The Window" with Cape Tribulation in the distance.

Tidal sand patterns of the Daintree estuary.

Prehistoric rainforest scene.

Overleaf: Pebbly Beach.

Morning twilight casts an enchanted glow onto the rainforest.

Peter Lik Galleries

Lik's original design concept was to create a contemporary space that enhances the natural beauty of his imagery, and the galleries continue to evolve under his direction. Attracting a diverse mix of visitors and collectors, the galleries are a fitting environment in which to experience an extraordinary photographic collection.

Each gallery offers the highest level of framing professionalism available and fully insures each piece, delivered to your doorstep worldwide.

A team of experienced Art Consultants are on hand to guide the visitor through their journey, or they can simply relax and enjoy the gallery at their leisure.

CAIRNS
4 Shields Street
Cairns Qld 4870 Australia
Telephone [07] 4031 8177
cairns@peterlik.com.au

LAHAINA
712 Front Street
Maui, Hawaii 96761 USA
Telephone [808] 661 6623
lahaina@peterlik.com

LAS VEGAS
Forum Shops at Caesars
3500 Las Vegas Blvd South
Las Vegas NV 89109 USA
Telephone [702] 836 3310
lasvegas@peterlik.com

NOOSA
Shop 2, Seahaven 9 Hastings Street
Noosa Heads Qld 4567 Australia
Telephone [07] 5474 8233
noosa@peterlik.com.au

PORT DOUGLAS
19 Macrossan Street
Port Douglas Qld 4871 Australia
Telephone [07] 4099 6050
port@peterlik.com.au

SYDNEY
Level 2 QVB
455 George Street Sydney
NSW 2000 Australia
Telephone [02] 9269 0182
sydney@peterlik.com.au

peterlik.com

Books by Peter Lik

- Australia
- Blue Mountains
- Brisbane
- Bundaberg
- Byron Bay
- Cairns
- Daintree and Cape Tribulation
- Fraser Island
- Gold Coast
- Great Barrier Reef
- Melbourne
- Port Douglas
- Sunshine Coast
- Sydney
- The Red Centre
- Townsville and Magnetic Island
- Whitsundays
- Wildlife
- World Heritage Rainforest

LARGE FORMAT PUBLICATIONS

- Australia - Images of a Timeless Land
- Spirit of America
- Las Vegas and Beyond
- Maui - Hawaiian Paradise